WOLVES

Published by Smart Apple Media
1980 Lookout Drive, North Mankato, Minnesota 56003

Design and Production by The Design Lab/Kathy Petelinsek

Photographs by Lynn M. Stone
Additional photographs by Tom Stack & Associates (2, 3, 15, 19, 22)

Library of Congress Cataloging-in-Publication Data
Gish, Melissa.
Wolves / by Melissa Gish
p. cm. – (Northern Trek)
Includes resources, glossary, and index
Summary: Describes the physical characteristics, behavior, habitat, life cycle,
and conservation of North American gray wolves.
ISBN 1-58340-037-0
1. Wolves–Juvenile literature. [1. Wolves.] I. Title. II. Series: Northern Trek (Mankato, Minn.)
QL737.C22G58   2000
599.773–dc21   99-39208
First Edition

2   4   6   8   9   7   5   3   1

NORTHERN TREK

WOLVES

WRITTEN BY MELISSA GISH
PHOTOGRAPHS BY LYNN M. STONE

SMART APPLE MEDIA

A full moon shines overhead. A lonesome howl. Then another, and another.

Soon a chorus of howls echoes through the darkness. For centuries these

cries were all people knew of the great wolves, one of the most feared of all

animals. The mere mention of its name kept people inside at night, their

doors and windows locked. Even today a fear of wolves remains, but new

studies are leading people to an understanding of this mysterious creature.

WOLVES ARE ONE of North America's most cunning and fierce **predators**, but they are also gentle, curious animals with strong family bonds. Almost all wolves belong to the species called gray wolf (*Canis lupus*). Only the red wolf (*Canis rufus*) of Mexico and the Southwest United States is different. Gray wolves have various names, depending on their **habitat**. For example, in northern Alaska and Canada they are called arctic wolves, and in northern Minnesota and Wisconsin they are called timber wolves.

A wolf is about the size of a German shepherd. Female wolves are generally 18 to 30 inches (46-76 cm) tall and weigh between 60 and 80 pounds (27-36 kg). Males are larger, at 30 to 36 inches (76-91 cm) tall and 75 to 100 pounds (34-45 kg). Like dogs, wolves bark, whimper, growl, and howl. Combined with body gestures, these sounds are their means of **communication**. Howling, for example, has many uses: to

---

A wolf's color helps it hide. Arctic wolves are white like snow, while timber wolves are dark gray or black like trees.

call for help, to express happiness or sadness, or to find a mate.

Because wolves live and hunt in packs—family groups of up to 20 members—communication is important, especially while hunting. The main prey of wolves are moose, deer, caribou, elk, and musk-oxen. These are all large hoofed animals capable of running long distances. A wolf can run at speeds of up to 40 miles (64 km) per hour and can chase prey for up to 20 miles (32 km). Despite this, wolves don't like to run after prey, as they usually cannot overtake it in a long chase. The best way for a wolf to hunt is by cooperating with its pack to trap its prey.

Of all wild dogs, which include foxes, coyotes, dingoes, and dholes, the gray wolf is the largest.

A wolf pack's territory can be from 50 to 150 square miles (130–389 km²). The boundaries are marked by piles of droppings and by urine sprayed on trees. The scent tells other wolves to stay away.

Wolves know that healthy prey may be too strong to bring down or may charge at the pack, so they often select animals that are either young, old, or sick. This actually helps the prey animals because it leaves more food for the stronger ones that will continue to populate the **herds**.

When the pack chooses a target, they begin to stalk it, silently creeping closer to it, low to the ground. They form a circle around the animal and may get as close as 30 feet (9 m) from it before being seen.

Packs cannot have more than 20 members, as hunting enough food to feed all members is too difficult.

Wolves have excellent peripheral vision, meaning they can quickly detect movement from the corners of their eyes. They can hear each other's howls up to three miles (4.8 km) away.

When the prey spots the wolves, instinct tells it to remain motionless. The pack of wolves stands very still too, watching the prey animal, waiting for it to move. Predator and prey may stare at each other for a long time before the prey finally makes a dash for escape. The wolves react instantly, tightening the circle around the animal until it has nowhere to go. Then they leap on it and bring it down.

Hunting is dangerous for wolves. Because a strong kick or a gouge from **antlers** can kill a wolf, it's important to stay away from the prey animal's head and hoofs. Wolves need to eat about 20 pounds (9 kg) of meat per feeding. When large prey is scarce, wolves will eat rabbits, beavers, and even mice.

Because hoofed animals **migrate** to find the grasses they eat, wolves must follow the herds—sometimes 40 to 60 miles (64-97 km) a day. Always, however, they return to their **territory** to raise families.

Wolves **breed** once per year. Once a mate is selected, the pair usually stays together for life. If one of the pair should die, its mate may never choose another. Pups are born two months after breeding. A few weeks before the pups arrive, the female digs a den. She chooses a spot on high ground near a river or stream. This way, the den is dry, but drinking water is nearby. When the pups

Wolves have 42 teeth—10 more than humans. Their four sharp canine teeth can grow to be two inches (5 cm) long.

are born, the male brings food to his mate. She will leave the den only to drink.

Between 3 and 13 dark brown or gray pups are born in a litter. They are deaf, and their eyes are closed. Each weighs only about one pound (0.5 kg). The pups grow quickly, nourished by their mother's milk. They will do nothing but sleep and **nurse** for the first three weeks. Then, when their eyes open, the pups will venture out of the den to meet their father and the rest of the pack.

From four to eight weeks, the pups, still nursing, begin to eat solid food. The adults chew up food for the pups. Finally, at about three months old, the pups will leave the den to sleep outside

From the moment they meet the other members of their pack, small pups are taught their place in the group.

The "Alpha male" is the pack leader. The "Alpha female" ranks just below him. Every wolf has its own rank in the pack. Young wolves are given their rank as they grow up. "Peripheral wolves" rank the lowest.

with the pack. They aren't yet old enough to join the hunts. Instead, they eat meat brought back by the adults to learn the taste of fresh prey.

For the first two years of its life, a young wolf will remain close to the pack. It will then decide whether to stay with its family or move away and become a "lone" wolf. A lone wolf is one that lives and hunts alone. It may eventually search for a mate to start its own pack, or it may join a smaller pack. A lone wolf usually cannot survive a winter on its own, as it needs the pack to successfully hunt.

Unlike domestic dogs, which are aloof and sometimes aggressive toward human strangers, wolves are gentle and curious. Traditionally, Native Americans respected the wolf for its family bonds and clever nature. White settlers in America, how-

ever, were frightened by wolves. Hunted and trapped in great numbers during the 1800s, wolves teetered on the brink of extinction.

Today, wolves are making a comeback. Ranchers still blame wolves for livestock killings, but in truth, wolves kill livestock only when their natural food supply is cut short by human interfer-ence. The U.S. Endangered Species Act of 1973 made it illegal to kill wolves, except in Alaska, where numbers are high. Wolves can once again thrive in North America, but only with the educa-tion and conservation efforts of people who recog-nize the wolf as a valuable part of nature.

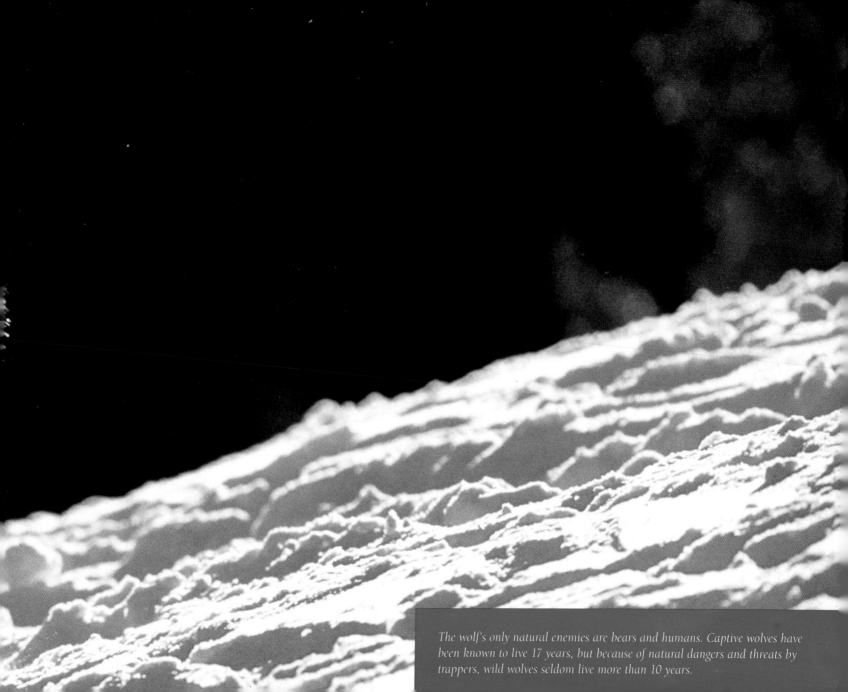

The wolf's only natural enemies are bears and humans. Captive wolves have been known to live 17 years, but because of natural dangers and threats by trappers, wild wolves seldom live more than 10 years.

UNLIKE MANY LARGE WILD

animals, such as buffalo or elk, it is rare for the general public to view the naturally shy wolf in an unprotected habitat. The best viewing areas are refuges and nature preserves that feature wolf packs.

Wolves are social animals, and those living in protected habitats often allow visitors to watch them in their family groups. Listed here are some gray wolf habitats with public access. As with any trek into nature, it is important to remember that wild animals are unpredictable and can be dangerous if approached. The best way to view wildlife is from a respectful—and safe—distance.

DENALI NATIONAL PARK IN ALASKA *Here is where the highest mountain in North America, Mt. McKinley, is found. This vast forest is home to numerous wolf packs, which hunt the area's abundant populations of Dall sheep and caribou.*

INTERNATIONAL WOLF CENTER IN ELY, MINNESOTA *Located in the Superior National Forest, the center features an exciting touch-and-see exhibit filled with activities and information, as well as an on-site wolf pack that visitors can study from an observation center. Contact www.wolf.org for info.*

BANFF NATIONAL PARK IN ALBERTA, CANADA *This huge wilderness area, Canada's oldest national park, is home to five wolf packs. The most likely places for visitors to spot wolves are near Lake Winnewanka and Lake Louise.*

ISLE ROYALE NATIONAL PARK IN HOUGHTON, MICHIGAN *Your chances of seeing wolves close-up in a deep woods setting are high in this area. For years, scientists have been studying the relationship between the wolf and moose populations here, and informative nature guides can help direct your hike.*

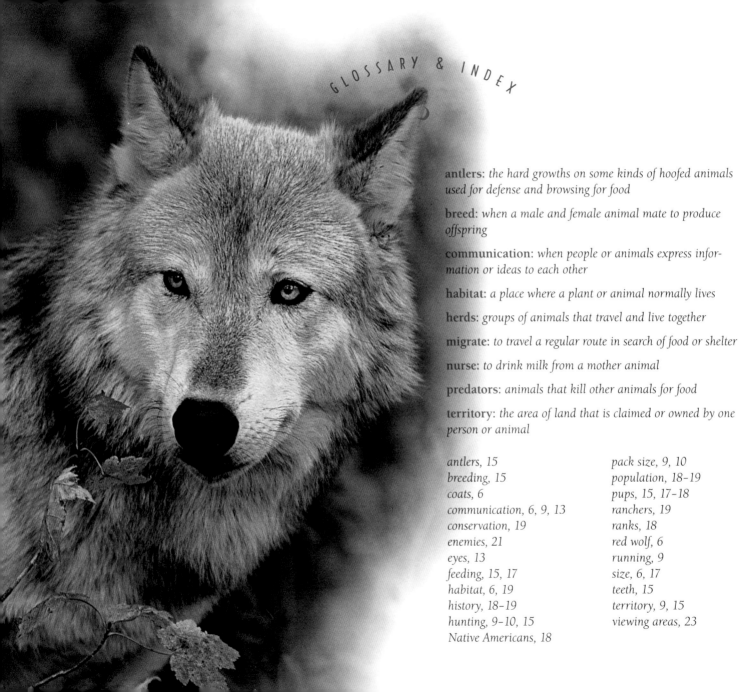

GLOSSARY & INDEX

antlers: *the hard growths on some kinds of hoofed animals used for defense and browsing for food*

breed: *when a male and female animal mate to produce offspring*

communication: *when people or animals express information or ideas to each other*

habitat: *a place where a plant or animal normally lives*

herds: *groups of animals that travel and live together*

migrate: *to travel a regular route in search of food or shelter*

nurse: *to drink milk from a mother animal*

predators: *animals that kill other animals for food*

territory: *the area of land that is claimed or owned by one person or animal*